DAILY LIFE

The American Revolution

Gregory T. Farshtey

**KIDHAVEN
PRESS™**

THOMSON

™

GALE

San Diego • Detroit • New York • San Francisco • Cleveland
New Haven, Conn. • Waterville, Maine • London • Munich

For more information, contact
KidHaven Press
27500 Drake Rd.
Farmington Hills, MI 48331-3535
Or you can visit our Internet site at http://www.gale.com

LIBRARY OF CONGRESS CATALOGING-IN-PUBLICATION DATA

Farshtey, Gregory T.
  The American Revolution / by Gregory T. Farshtey.
    p. cm.—(Daily life)
Summary: Discusses daily home life during the American Revolution, equipment used by the Continental and British armies, and training methods of both armies. Includes bibliographical references and index.
  ISBN 0-7377-1402-6 (lib. bdg. : alk. paper)
  1. United States—History—Revolution, 1775–1783—Juvenile literature [1. United States—History—Revolution, 1775–1783.] I. Title. II. Series.
  E208 .F37 2003
  973 .3—dc21

                                                     2002006298

Printed in China

Contents

CHAPTER ONE

Life During the American Revolution

More than 2.5 million people were living in the American colonies when the American Revolution began in 1775. All but a few hundred of them lived in the thirteen colonies, a narrow strip of land that extended from Maine to Georgia. Colonists had come to America from different countries in search of new opportunity. But during and after the Revolutionary War, their lives changed in many ways.

City Life and Country Life

Nine out of every ten colonial families lived in the country, and many of them were farmers. The war created new problems, new chances to make money, and a major change in how the farms were run and who did most of the work.

Before the war began, men did the outdoor chores on the farm: planting, harvesting, building and repairing fences, tending to livestock, and more. Women were responsible for domestic jobs, such as making food and clothes, and doing the cleaning. But when the war began, men left to join the Continental army. As a result, their wives had to take over running the farms. For women, this meant a lot more work and greater responsibility. It also gave women a chance to show that they could make important decisions and work the land just as well as their husbands had.

A woman concentrates on spinning yarn in this historical portrayal of colonial times.

Having armies on the march changed life for farmers. Both the British and the Continental armies needed food, and neighboring farms were the best place to get it. For the British, the only fresh food they could get came from local farms because all the rest of their food came by ship from England. Sometimes, soldiers from both sides of the war would pay local farmers for food. The farmers could make a good profit from these sales. In fact, American general Nathanael Greene complained

Colonists make their way through a busy street in New York City during the 1700s.

that some farmers were charging as much as four times what their crops were worth.

Armies were not always willing to pay for what they wanted. British troops would often raid farms they thought belonged to rebels. They took whatever they could carry and burned the rest.

Each city was affected differently by the war. For example, the British occupied Philadelphia for nine months, but the city suffered little as a result. No battles were fought there, and the British eventually marched out peacefully.

Life in New York City was quite different. The British occupied New York City from 1776 to 1783, and conditions were terrible. Food and fuel were in short supply, refugees packed the city, and British soldiers enforced harsh laws. Overcrowding and poor conditions led to disease. Much of the city was in ruins because of a huge fire that broke out shortly after the British took over. Captured rebels and those who supported them were kept in churches which were used as jails. Other prisoners were kept on a prison ship anchored off Brooklyn. Prisoners spent the war there, with no hope of getting out. Meanwhile, the citizens of the colonies dealt with all the other changes brought by the Revolution.

Money and Goods

Before the war began, many essential goods were shipped to America from England or from England's other colonies around the world. When the war began, those shipments stopped and shortages became a problem. Colonists lacked sugar, pepper, coffee, shoes, and pins, among other things.

A government official bows to leaders of the Continental Congress before a session begins.

The lack of pins was a particular problem. Women sewed clothes for their families, and new clothing from England was no longer available. John Adams's wife, Abigail, insisted that her husband send pins from Philadelphia. "The cry for pins is so great that what we used to buy for 7 shillings and sixpence are now 20 shillings and not to be had for that,"[1] she wrote.

Another problem for the colonists was money. The money used in the colonies had been the British pound. But after the war began, the **Continental Congress** decided America should issue its own money. It authorized the printing of paper money called continentals.

Merchants in the colonies did not trust this new money, though. Many considered British pounds valuable and continentals worthless. As the war went on, continentals lost even more of their value.

Farmers loyal to the king and shopkeepers refused to accept the new continentals. "I do not like your rebel money,"[2] one tavern owner told American general Israel Putnam. Even merchants who supported the American cause were more willing to sell their goods to the British, who paid in pounds. (As late as the 1940s, Americans used the phrase "not worth a continental" to describe something they thought was worthless.)

Patriots Versus Loyalists

Patriots supported the U.S. cause and wanted independence from England. Loyalists supported Britain and its king, George III. Because patriots and loyalists were on opposite sides of the Revolution, great conflict was created within communities. For example if the majority of citizens in a town were patriots, loyalists' houses were burned, their goods taken, and they were banished from the town. The same happened to patriots in towns controlled by the British and their loyalist supporters. It mattered little if a next-door neighbor had been a friend for many years. If he chose to support the other side, he was an enemy and a traitor.

How a patriot or loyalist was treated in his town depended completely on which army was in the neighborhood. When Washington and the Continental army held New Jersey, citizens lined up to swear their loyalty to the American cause. When the British later marched in and took over the same area, citizens lined up to take back their oaths and swear allegiance to King George III. If the British were nearby, mobs of loyalists might attack the homes of rebels; if the Continental army was marching through, mobs of patriots might do the same thing to loyalists' homes.

Many loyalists lost their houses and property to the colonies they lived in because of laws that were passed stripping them of their rights. These loyalists became refugees and streamed into New York, Philadelphia, and other cities held by the British. Unfortunately, the British did not have the extra food or supplies to take care of all these people.

Patriot families also had to move as the war shifted back and forth. When British ships controlled Boston Harbor and the waters along the coastline, many colonial families

Actors dressed as loyalists carefully aim their rifles as another plays the fife behind them.

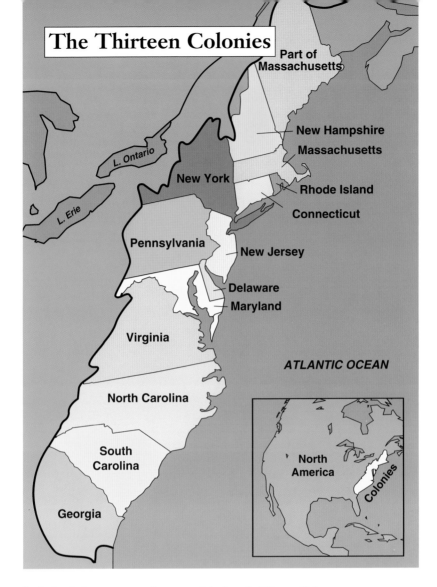

The Thirteen Colonies

Part of Massachusetts

New Hampshire

Massachusetts

L. Ontario

New York

Rhode Island

L. Erie

Connecticut

Pennsylvania

New Jersey

Delaware

Maryland

Virginia

ATLANTIC OCEAN

North Carolina

South Carolina

North America

Colonies

Georgia

left their homes and moved inland. They did not return until the British abandoned Boston. Even wealthy landowners could lose their homes. The British often burned the grand homes of rich patriots as punishment for their rebellion.

After the war was over, most colonies restored loyalists' property to them. But America needed time to heal the division between patriot and loyalist, while the number of loyalists who fled the country meant a shortage of workers in the new nation.

CHAPTER TWO

The Continental Army

The posters were seen all over town. Brave, healthy, and able-bodied men were needed to enlist in the new Continental army, they said, to fight for American freedom. When the struggle was over, the potential recruit was told, he would return home a hero with his pockets full of money.

The first shots of the American Revolution had been fired only two months before in April 1775, in Lexington, Massachusetts. Relations between England and its American colonies had been worsening for some time. The British government wanted the colonies to help pay for their own defense, and so it created many new taxes for the colonists to pay. Because the colonists had no say in the government's decisions, they did not want to pay the taxes. The British finally sent troops to the colonies to enforce the laws. The colonists grew even more upset and began preparing to defend their homes and communities against the British.

American **militia** fought the first battles. These were ordinary citizens who assembled during an emergency. Just about every town had a militia for defense against attacks by Native Americans or other threats. But once the war began, it became obvious that the colonies needed an army of their own to stand against the thousands of British troops

George Washington, pictured here in military dress, was elected by the Continental Congress to lead the Continental army.

who had come to crush the rebellion. The Continental Congress voted to create a Continental army, commanded by General George Washington.

Deciding to form an army was easy. Finding men willing to leave their homes, families, and businesses for months at a time to join that army was much more difficult.

Recruiting for the Continental Army

The recruitment posters nailed up in towns and villages throughout the colonies made joining the Continental army sound like a great idea. Any man who enlisted would get a **bounty**, a small amount of cash just for signing up. He was also promised a salary every year, plus clothing and plenty of food. This offer, combined with the patriotic feelings many had in 1775, inspired men to join the army, though not as many as Washington would have liked. The volunteers signed papers that committed them to the army until the end of the year, and then they would be free to return home.

The men who joined the Continental army at the beginning of the war were giving up a great deal by enlisting. Many of the early recruits were farmers or other men with businesses of their own. While they were serving in the army, their wives or other relatives had to look after their property and businesses. Still, most Americans believed that the war would not last long. Most Americans thought that the British would make peace by 1776 rather than risk losing the colonies.

Instead, the war went on until 1783 and it became harder to find men to join the army. As time passed, fewer men with farms or other property to look after en-

The age of a Revolutionary War soldier varied greatly, as portrayed by this group in Virginia.

listed. The Continental army became home to the colonies' poor, as well as to young men who had not yet made their fortune in life. Most soldiers were in their twenties, but some regiments had drummer boys as young as ten and soldiers as old as seventy-two.

Many African Americans also joined the Continental army. Roughly thirty thousand African Americans, most of them slaves, fought for independence even though they were not regarded as citizens and had no rights under the law. Many of these men were sent to the army as substitutes for their masters, who had been drafted but chose not to fight. In return for their service in the army, these slaves were promised their freedom. Many settled in the northern states after the war was over.

Toward the end of the war, the offer made to recruits became more generous. Bounties were increased and men were promised one hundred acres of land once the war ended. But those who signed up quickly discovered that life in the army was very different from the heroic picture painted by the recruiting posters.

Life in the Continental Army

The Continental army faced many challenges in the Revolutionary War. The men were not professional soldiers and did not have the training they needed. They were also heavily outnumbered by the British army.

But the most difficult obstacle the Continental army had to overcome was a lack of food, clothing, and other supplies. Many colonial merchants preferred selling their goods to the British, who paid more, so shortages were common. Hunger and fatigue made the soldiers' lives even more difficult. As Joseph Plumb Martin, a soldier from Connecticut, wrote, "We had a hard duty to perform and little or no strength to perform it with."[3]

Lack of food forced the soldiers to eat whatever they could. Martin reported that he had seen men roast and eat their own shoes, and he himself had eaten birch bark. One Thanksgiving, the holiday dinner for the men was less than a cup of rice and a tablespoon of vinegar.

A shortage of clothing and boots was a huge problem as well, especially in the winter. Martin wrote that most of the men were "not only shirtless and barefoot, but destitute of all other clothing, especially blankets. I procured a small piece of raw cowhide and made myself a pair of **moccasins**, which kept my feet from the frozen ground."[4]

Generals Lafayette (left) and Washington (right) discuss the harsh conditions at Valley Forge as a group of soldiers huddles for warmth.

Volunteer soldiers wait for the order to fire from Colonel William Prescott (with sword) just before the Battle of Bunker Hill.

He went on to say that the men who were forced to go barefoot ended up with bleeding feet. They could be tracked by blood in the snow.

Despite all these hardships, the men continued to fight until the war was won. Some fought out of patriotism; some, to defend their homes and families; some, for personal pride; and some, for the money and a chance to make something of themselves. Against huge odds, they defeated the British. But how did a poorly supplied, badly trained force do that?

How the Continental Army Won the War

General George Washington knew his army was not large enough or strong enough to win many head-to-head battles with the British. His war plan from the start was to keep his army whole while wearing down the British. His plan involved three strategies.

The first of the strategies was to keep on the move. Washington's biggest fear was that the British would surround his army and he would be forced to surrender. One way to avoid that was to keep moving. Because Washington had fewer men and supplies than the British, and because his troops knew the country better, they were able to move faster than the enemy.

The second of the strategies was to avoid huge battles. Washington knew that it would take only one or two big losses in battle to severely weaken or wipe out his army. To avoid this, he staged hit-and-run attacks with the Continental army. After a quick skirmish, the army slipped away in the dark before the British could catch them.

A painting depicts the gruesome Battle of Princeton when a British soldier stabbed American general Hugh Mercer (far left) in 1777.

The third and final of these strategies was to make the war drag on. The longer the Continental army was intact, the longer the war would last. Washington believed if the war lasted for years, the British government and the British people would get tired of it and want to stop fighting. By staying on the move and not giving the British the chance for a quick victory, Washington helped make it possible for the Continental army to win the war.

However, for any of these strategies to be effective, Washington's army first required men, and the training needed to turn these men into soldiers.

CHAPTER THREE

Equipment and Training

A new recruit to the Continental army usually arrived in camp with a gun he brought from home, the clothes on his back, and very little military training. His weapon, how well he used it, and how well he could work together with his fellow soldiers were vital to America's chances of winning the Revolutionary War.

To Arms!

A colonial soldier normally carried a **musket**, a hatchet, and ammunition. Muskets were difficult to use in battle. They took a very long time to load, and when fired they created a big cloud of smoke. After a few shots, it became almost impossible to see at what—or at whom—he was shooting. Continental soldier Corporal John Munroe recalled a battle in which, after two rounds were fired, "the smoke prevented our seeing anything but the heads of some of the British horses."[5]

Being unable to see the target made it hard to hit anything. But that was not the only reason that shots fired by both sides missed their targets so often. Muskets were not very accurate weapons. A soldier had to be within about fifty yards of the target to have a chance of hitting it. In most battles, soldiers lined up and marched toward each other until they were close enough to shoot. It was considered a sign of courage and honor for a soldier to wait until the other side had fired first before shooting his own weapon.

Patriots steady themselves with their muskets and wait as British troops approach.

Despite a poor weapon and thick smoke, soldiers should still have been able to hit their targets if they aimed carefully. But soldiers on both sides of the war rarely ever aimed before firing. British soldiers were actually trained to look away from their target before shooting, so that the flash of the gun firing would not blind them. Soldiers were expected to load, fire, and reload as quickly as possible during a battle. They were not expected to take the time to aim.

Ready, Load . . . Fire?

Loading a musket was a twelve-step process. A musket cartridge was a piece of paper with black powder and a lead musket ball inside. To load the musket, the soldier had to first bite off the end of the cartridge. Doing this almost always resulted in the soldier getting a little bit of black powder on his mouth or face. After a battle, one could always tell the men who had actually fired their weapons because their faces were dirty.

The soldier would then pour a little of the black powder into the **pan.** Once that was done, he would stuff the cartridge into the muzzle of the rifle and ram it down. When he pulled the trigger of the musket, a piece of metal called a firing cock would fall, striking a piece of **flint** against steel. This made a spark that ignited the black powder in the pan. The musket would then fire the musket ball.

Any of these steps could go wrong and cause injury. If a soldier fired into the wind, his face might be burned by a backfire. If it were raining or snowing, the black powder would get damp and not ignite. Muskets were

An actor squeezes his eyes shut to protect himself from his musket's spark and smoke.

almost useless in the rain or snow, because with damp powder they would not fire at all.

American soldiers also had some problems with the musket that the British did not: a shortage of the materials needed to make the weapon work. Musket balls were made of lead, but at the start of the war only a few deposits of lead had been found in the colonies. Lead was stripped off of roofs and rain spouts and melted down into lead bars that were given to the troops. The soldiers would then melt down the bars to make musket balls. Some colonists even melted a statue of King George III to make ammunition for the army!

Flint was also in short supply. A piece of flint lasted for about sixty musket shots before it had to be replaced. But the stone was scarce, and few skilled stonemasons could shape the flint so it would fit in the musket.

Finally, gunpowder was scarce as well. The shortages were so bad that in 1776 Benjamin Franklin suggested that American soldiers should be armed with bows and arrows! Franklin believed that four arrows could be fired in the same time it would take to make one musket shot, and that the enemy would be distracted by the sight of flying arrows.

In spite of the Continental army's problems with weapons most soldiers had experience loading and firing guns, either from their local militia or from time spent hunting for game. But other important skills soldiers needed required special training.

Training to Be a Soldier

Different types of colonial troops trained in different ways. Before the war, militia units usually had two small drills a year. They would meet in the center of the town and practice marching, loading, and firing. Once a year, militias from neighboring towns would get together for a large drill. After the war began, many of the militia units became part of the Continental army, and they trained more often.

The minutemen were a special group of militia men. As their name indicates, their job was to be ready for action in sixty seconds. In time of crisis, a minuteman might sleep in his clothes, with his musket and other gear close by. Minutemen had to take a great deal of time away from their farms or businesses to train. They were

Some colonists use their muskets as clubs after having run out of ammunition during battle.

A minuteman hastily prepares to leave for war as his family watches his departure with dread.

expected to drill as much as two and a half days per week, even in harsh winter weather. "I have spent many an evening going through the exercise drill on the barn floor with my mittens on,"[6] wrote one minuteman.

Minutemen had to learn up to fifty different battlefield commands. They also practiced firing in three rows, with the first row kneeling and the other two standing. Being able to reload and fire as quickly as possible could mean the difference between victory and defeat, so that was practiced often.

A drummer and fife player march in front of Continental soldiers who are completing drill exercises.

Continental army soldiers trained mostly during the winter for two reasons. First, because of snow and ice, it was very hard to move troops and supplies during the winter, so armies would camp until spring. With no battles to fight or marches to make, they had time to train. Second, General Washington liked to keep his men on a regular training schedule in camp, regardless of the weather conditions. He wanted to instill discipline and keep them busy.

Continental army training included not only how to march together and obey complicated orders, but also how to keep a clean camp and how to treat officers with respect. Soldiers were awakened at three in the morning and marched around the camp, then drilled on how to handle their muskets, load quickly, and fire in a **volley**. Soldier Joseph Plumb Martin wrote that every day, whenever he did not have other duties, he would be drilling.

In the end, all that training helped the Continental army look and fight like a professional army. That helped to boost the spirits of the men and keep them going despite all the hardships of war.

CHAPTER FOUR

The British Army

As the Revolutionary War began, the odds of victory favored the British. They were better armed, better supplied, better trained, and better disciplined than the colonial troops, and there were many more of them. They were led by experienced generals and backed by one of the most powerful navies in the world. With all this on their side, most British officers believed the war would be over in a year and the colonies would be back under England's rule once again.

This did not go according to plan, however. The war dragged on for eight years, and in the end the British surrendered. How could the British lose a war they seemed so certain to win easily? In many ways, the British made things worse for themselves.

British Officers

Movies and television always show the British army as a highly trained group of professional soldiers, marching in a straight line across the battlefield. That picture is very close to the truth. But what they do not show is the kind of men who made up that army, and how they got to be so disciplined.

The generals and other high-ranking officers in the British army came from wealthy families. Money was used to gain the honor of joining a particular regiment

Actors dressed as British soldiers march to battle and proudly display their country's flag.

or to achieve a promotion. Because it was almost impossible to save money on low army pay, an officer had to have money of his own if he wanted to advance. Wealth, more than wisdom or battle experience, dictated who led a British regiment into combat.

Actors dressed as colonials make shoes by hand. Officers and troops in both the British and Continental armies had experience with many trades.

Many British officers looked down on the men who led the Continental army. The colonial officers were all working men and so were regarded as lower class by the British. After capturing some American troops, one British officer wrote, "Of those we took, one major was a blacksmith, another a hatter. Of their captains, there was a butcher, a tanner, a shoe-maker, a tavern-keeper, etc. Yet they pretended to be gentlemen."[7]

The British officers came from the upper classes of society, but their troops came from the very bottom. Many British soldiers were thieves, outcasts, or the poorest of the poor, recruited from prisons and slums. Some joined the army because it was a choice between eating or starving or, worse, hanging for some minor offense. Others were "recruited" while drunk in a tavern and woke up the next day to find themselves in the military.

Heavy Uniforms and Heavy Equipment

These men lived a hard life. Discipline in the army was brutal, and any violation of the rules was punished by lashes with a whip. Pay was very small, and portions of the cost of food, uniforms, medicine, transportation, and involuntary contributions were deducted before the soldier ever saw his money.

Life was difficult off the battlefield, but it was even more challenging in combat. In addition to a heavy uniform that featured a red coat made of wool and a hat made of bearskin, British soldiers also carried an ammunition pouch, a cartridge box, and a **haversack** containing extra clothes, provisions, a canteen, and camp tools. When fully dressed and equipped, a British soldier carried

125 pounds on his back! That would be like carrying a small man on his shoulders as he marched.

Supplying the army while it was in America was a problem as well. All supplies, including meat, had to come three thousand miles by ship. Vessels were often lost in storms or from attacks by American ships. This distance between America and England also meant it took a long time for messages to go back and forth between British generals and their superiors in London.

Despite these disadvantages the British army was respected and feared around the world. Their secret weapon was the bayonet charge. Hundreds of soldiers would charge an enemy position, shouting and screaming, then attack using their razor-sharp bayonets. Only the very bravest enemy soldiers would not break and run when they saw a bayonet charge coming their way.

A Different Way of Fighting

But British troops found the war in the colonies to be very different from any other they had experienced. European wars were all fought between two armies facing each other across an open field, and so were most Revolutionary War battles. But American sharpshooters would also fire from up in trees or behind rocks, usually targeting British officers first.

The British had also counted on a large portion of the colonists to help and support them out of loyalty to the king. In fact, only about a third of the colonists were loyalists. They were scattered and often afraid to show their support for the British, for their neighbors might drive them from their homes.

A large number of colonists were neutral about the war and supported whichever side seemed to be winning. But when the British attempted to start a slave revolt in the south and recruited Native American tribes to

British soldiers defend themselves with their bayonets in this depiction of the Boston Massacre, a riot that ended with the death of five colonists.

fight for them in the north, many of these neutrals were angered and decided to support the rebels.

Too Big a Country, Too Few Men

When British troops sailed across the Atlantic toward the colonies, they knew they would be facing more than just the militia and the Continental army when

The British army traditionally fought in straight lines across a field, as shown in this reenactment of a Revolutionary War battle.

Colonists chase British troops off a bridge.

they reached shore. The colonies stretched over a vast amount of land, much of it wilderness, with few good roads and plenty of places for an enemy to hide. The colonists knew their land and how to pick the best places for a fight. The British would have to adjust to the hard traveling, the weather, and the long-distance marches in search of the Continentals.

British general Charles Cornwallis (standing, center) surrenders to George Washington and the Continental army in Yorktown, Virginia, in 1781.

The size of the country was a particularly difficult problem for the British because they did not have enough men in the army. At the beginning of the war, British general William Howe said it would take thirty thousand men to stop the rebellion in Massachusetts. But Britain did not have anywhere near that many men available to go to North America. Their army was scattered around the world, from England and Ireland to Gibraltar and the West Indies.

The British government's solution was to hire men from other countries to fight on England's side in the war. They first asked Russia for twenty thousand men, but Russia said no. So England turned to Germany instead, hiring close to thirty thousand men, known as **Hessians.** The name came from the region of Germany called Hesse-Cassel, where most of the men came from.

The Hessians were skilled soldiers, but they also caused some problems for the British. The Hessians looted towns after a battle. Because they did not speak English, they could not tell the rebel colonists from those loyal to King George III. Often, they would rob the houses of people who were on England's side in the war.

Eventually, the lack of available fighting men, the high cost of fighting the war in America, and a loss of support among the British people for the war forced the British to surrender.

Notes

Chapter One: Life During the American Revolution

1. Quoted in David McCullough, *John Adams.* New York: Simon and Schuster, 2001, p. 21.

2. Quoted in Henry Steele Commager and Richard B. Morris, eds. *The Spirit of 'Seventy-Six.* Edison, NJ: Castle Books, 2002, p. 790.

Chapter Two: The Continental Army

3. *The Diary of Joseph Plumb Martin.* http://mrbooth.com.

4. *The Diary of Joseph Plumb Martin.*

Chapter Three: Equipment and Training

5. Quoted in Richard Wheeler, *Voices of 1776: The Story of the American Revolution in the Words of Those Who Were There.* New York: Meridian, 1972, p. 7.

6. Quoted in Thomas Fleming, *Liberty! The American Revolution.* New York: Viking, 1997, p. 107.

Chapter Four: The British Army

7. Quoted in Wheeler, *Voices of 1776,* p. 86.

Glossary

bounty: A reward given for performing a service. The Continental army paid men a bounty for enlisting.

Continental Congress: Representatives of the thirteen American colonies who governed the country during the Revolutionary War.

flint: A very hard type of rock, usually gray, which produces sparks when struck with steel.

haversack: A canvas bag used to carry gear, usually worn over one shoulder.

Hessians: German soldiers hired by the British to fight in the Revolutionary War.

loyalists: Residents of the American colonies who remained loyal to King George III during the war. Also called Tories.

militia: Military units made up of citizen volunteers, rather than professional soldiers.

moccasins: Slippers made from soft leather. Moccasins were originally worn by Native Americans.

musket: A firearm used by British and American troops, slow to load and not very accurate.

pan: The part of the musket that held a small amount of gunpowder. When the trigger was pulled, a piece of flint struck a piece of steel, producing sparks. The sparks would cause the gunpowder in the pan to ignite, and the weapon would fire.

patriots: People who fought for independence from England during the American Revolution.

volley: Shots fired by a number of guns at the same time.

For Further Exploration

Books

Christopher Collier, *The American Revolution, 1763–1783.* Tarrytown, NY: Benchmark Books, 1998. An overview of the causes of the American Revolution and a history of the war.

Edward F. Dolan, *The American Revolution: How We Fought the War of Independence.* Brookfield, CT: Millbrook Press, 1995. Takes readers through the American Revolution from Lexington to Yorktown, with profiles of famous figures of the war.

David King, *Benedict Arnold and the American Revolution.* Woodbridge, CT: Blackbirch Press, 1998. A biography of the infamous American traitor who planned to surrender West Point to the British.

Kay Moore and Daniel O'Leary, *If You Lived at the Time of the American Revolution.* New York: Scholastic Trade, 1998. An easy-to-follow look at life during the Revolution, with a special focus on children in the colonies.

Diane Silcox-Jarrett, *Heroines of the American Revolution: America's Founding Mothers.* Chapel Hill, NC: Green Angel Press, 1998. Short biographies of famous women of the American Revolution.

Websites

Liberty! The American Revolution (www.pbs.org). This website offers timelines and resource material, a

Revolutionary War game, and a look at daily life during the Revolutionary War era.

The History Place (www.historyplace.com). An overview of American history from the early colonial era through the American Revolution and the birth of the United States of America.

Index

Picture Credits

About the Author

Gregory T. Farshtey is the author of more than thirty books, including three novels and a number of children's game books. A graduate of the State University of New York at Geneseo, Mr. Farshtey is employed as a writer for a major children's magazine and website. When not writing or reading, he relaxes with his wife Lisa and their two cats in Rocky Hill, Connecticut.